HOW TO DO N

SIT BACK & RELAX TO YOUR HEART'S CONTENT

Master The Art of Relaxation To Recharge Your Body And Mind

ROBIN RHODES

Table of Contents

Chapter 1:
Happy People Live Slow

"Slow Living means **structuring your life around meaning and fulfilment**. Similar to 'voluntary simplicity and 'downshifting,' it emphasizes a **less-is-more approach**, focusing on the quality of your life…Slow Living addresses the desire to lead a more balanced life and pursue a **more holistic sense of well-being** in the fullest sense of the word. In addition to the personal advantages, there are potential **environmental benefits** as well. When we slow down, we often use fewer resources and produce less waste, both of which have a lighter impact on the earth."

Slow living is a state of mind it will make you feel purposeful and is more fulfilling. It is all about being consistent and steady. Now that you have an idea of slow living, we will break down some myths attached to slow living and how to start slow living for mind peace and happiness. The first myth is that slow living is about doing everything as slowly as possible. Slow living is not about doing everything in slow motion but doing things at the right speed and not rushing. It is all about gaining time so you can do things that are important to you. The second myth is that slow living is the same as simple living. Now simple living is more worldly, and simple living is more focused on time.

The third myth is that slow living is an aesthetic that you see on desaturated Instagram posts, but that is not true; this is considered a minimalist aesthetic, whereas slow living is a minimalist lifestyle. The 4th myth is that slow living is about doing and being less. That is not at all true. It is all about removing the non-essentials from your life so you can have more time to be yourself. And the last myth is that slow living is anti-technology now. This is not about travelling back in time but all about using tech as a tool and not vice versa.

If you like this idea of living, we are going to list ten ways in which you can start slow living;

1. Define what is most important to you(essentials)
2. Say no to everything else (non-essentials)
3. Understand busyness and that it is a choice
4. Create space and margin in your day and life
5. Practice being present
6. Commit to putting your life before work
7. Adopt a slow information diet
8. Get outside physically and connect dots mentally
9. Start slow and small by downshifting
10. Find inspiration in the slow living community

Sit back and think about what the purpose of your life is, what you ultimately want from your life and not just in a monetary sense. Think about what you would like for your lifestyle to be 50 years from now, and then start working on it today. Suppose you have not figured out the purpose. In that case, there are multiple personality tests available on the internet that will help you determine your personality type and then eventually help you create your purpose.

Chapter 2:

How to Deal with Stress Head On? 7 Things You Can Start Today

Drop your shoulders, release your tongue from your palate. Unclench your teeth and let your brows relax. You see, this is how stressed you are all the time, you forget completely about how it is affecting your body.

In this roaring river of the 21st century, we are all feeling the tide rising and falling 24/7. It will be a white lie if any of you claim to never feel stressed. We are all under varying degrees of stress all the time.

So what is stress exactly? Stress is not merely a stimulus or a physical response of our bodies but a process by which we appraise and cope with environmental threats and challenges. When expressed in short bursts or taken as a challenge, stressors may have positive effects. However, if stress is threatening or prolonged, it can be harmful for us.

So how then do we handle it?

It seems like quite a drag for most of us and pretty annoying a lot of the time, but here are several ways we can deal with it and come out of it stronger than before.

7 Tips to Deal with stress and anxiety

Number 1: Go To Bed Early and Wake up Early

Have you heard the quote "Early to Bed, early to rise, makes a man healthy, wealthy and wise."? When was the last time you went to sleep early? I believe that going to bed early is something we all know we need to do but hardly ever do.

Starting your day off early has many wonderful biological effects. Mornings tend to be cool, silent, serene, and distraction-free. This calmness helps bring our stress levels down and prepares us for the day ahead. By practicing some deep breathing techniques in the morning, it will also aid in flow and circulation throughout our bodies, something that is good for the mind and soul.

Number 2: Start Practicing Yoga or meditation

Yoga and meditation, while they are two separate practices, they overlap in many key areas. Yoga poses are great for us to engage with our bodies, to stretch out our muscles, tight sections of our bodies, and to help us focus on our breath at all times. Each yoga pose targets a unique meridian of our bodies, many allowing us to release tensions that might otherwise have built up without realizing. You can try simple poses such as a child pose or shavasana, or downward dog, to get yourself started.

Meditation on the other hand focuses stilling the mind through focus on the breath as well. Letting our thoughts flow freely, we are able to acknowledge the stressors we face without judgement. Try out some guided mindfulness meditation practices to get your started.

Number 3: Having Proper Time Management

Many of us overlook the importance of proper time management. We often let our crazy schedules overwhelm us. By being unorganized with our time, we are also unorganized with our emotions. If we let our calendar be filled with chaos, there is no doubt that we will feel like chaos as well. Stress levels will be bound to rise. Have proper blocks of time dedicated to each task in your day. Trust me you will feel a whole lot more in control of everything.

Number 4: Make time for your hobbies

We should all strive to live a happy and balanced life. If work is the only thing on our agenda, we will have no outlet to destress, relax, recharge, and be ready to face new challenges that might tax our physical and mental abilities.

Whatever your hobbies are: baking, tennis, crafting, surfboarding, or even shopping, as long as you plan them in your schedule and do them, you will definitely feel a whole lot better about everything. Let out all the steam, stress, anxieties, as you engage in your hobbies, or even just forget about them for a minute. Give yourself the space to breathe and just enjoy doing the fun things in life. Life isn't just all about work. Play is equally important too.

Number 5: Music is food for your soul

Music has many therapeutic qualities. If you feel your stress levels rising, consider popping your earbuds into your ears and playing your favorite songs on spotify. If you are looking for calm, you may want to consider listening to some chill music as well.

The kind of your music you listen to will have a direct effect on your mood and the way you feel. So choose your playlists wisely. Don't go heavy metal or goth, unless of course it helps calm you down.

Number 6: Start Cleaning your clutter

This may seem like I am quoting a movie where the stressed teenage girl decides to clean her room when she is feeling low. I'd say movies are made out of someone's real experience.

Cleaning your room or clutter can be one of the best therapies.

A messy space is a recipe for anxiety and stress. When we see clutter, we feel cluttered. Once you clear all the stuff you don't need, you will feel much lighter instantly.

Number 7: Allow nature to heal you

Nature is amusing and wonderful. Everything in nature is closer to our basic making than anything that we are dealing with today. So try getting close to nature, it will make you feel relaxed and at the same time enable you to enrich your brain.

Watch the sun setting into the sky and wake up to look at the colors at dawn.
There is nothing more beautiful in this world that we get to experience every single day no matter where we are on this earth.

Take a stroll in your favourite park, go for a cycle, a jog, or even just a stroll with your pet. Allow nature to melt away your stress and bring your peace.

Final Thoughts

Stressors are a part of life. Something we cannot escape from. But if we put in place some healthy habits and practices, we can reduce and release those negativities from our bodies, cleansing us to take on more stress in the future.

Chapter 3:
How To Achieve True Happiness

How many of us actually know what happiness really is? And how many of us spend our whole lives searching for it but never seem to be happy?

I want to share with you my story today of how i stumbled upon true happiness and how you can achieve the same for yourself in your life.

Many of us go through the motion of trying to earn money because we think the more money we have, the better our lives will be. We chase the dream of increasing our earning power so that we can afford to buy nicer and more expensive things. And we believe that when we have more money, our happiness level will increase as well and we will be filled with so much money and happiness that we can finally stop chasing it.

Now I just wanna say, Yes, for those who come from a not so affluent background where they have a family to feed and basic needs have to be met to in order for them to survive, having a monetary goal to work towards is truly commendable as their drive, motivation, and sole purpose comes from supporting their family. Their sense of achievement, joy, and happiness comes from seeing their loved ones attaining basic needs and then go on to achieve success later in life at the expense of their time and energy. But they are more than okay with that and they do so with a willing heart, mind, and soul. You might even say that these people have achieved true happiness. Not because they are chasing more money, but because they are using that money to serve a greater purpose other than themselves.

But what about the rest of us who seemingly have everything we could ever want but never seem to be happy? We work hard at our jobs every single day waiting for our next promotion so that we can command a higher pay. And as our income grows, so does our appetite and desire for more expensive material things.

For guys we might chase that fancy new watch like rolex, omega, breitling, drooling over that model that always seem to be on a never-ending waitlist. And as we purchased one, feeling that temporary joy and satisfaction, we quickly look towards that next model as the shiny object we have starts to slowly fade. We lose our so-called happiness in time and We go back to work dreaming about that next watch just to feel that joy and excitement again. This could apply to other material things such as a shiny new technology gadgets smartphones, tv, and even cars.

For women, while might not be true for everyone, They might look towards that designer shoe, that branded handbag, ar that fancy jewellery that costs thousands of dollars to purchase but happily pay for it because they think it makes them feel better about ourselves. Or they could even use these purchases as retail therapy from their stressful lives and jobs.

Whatever these expensive purchases may be, we think that by spend our hard earned money on material things, it will bring us happiness and joy, but somehow it never does, and in most cases it is only temporary satisfactions.

That was exactly what happened with me. I kept chasing a higher income thinking it would bring me happiness. As a lover of technology, I always sought to buy the latest gadgets I could get my hands on. The excitement peaks and then fades. For me I realised that I had created an endless loop of trying to chase happiness but always coming up short.

One day I sat down and reflected on what exactly made me REALLY happy and I started writing down a list.

My List Came down to these in no particular order: Spending time with family, spending time with friends, helping others, having a purpose in life, being at peace with myself, working on my own dreams, singing and making music, exercising, being grateful, and finally being a loving person to others.

As I went through this list, I realised that hey, in none of the list did i write "making more money" or "buying more things". And it finally dawned on me that these are REALLY the things that made me truly happy. And only after I had defined these things did i actively choose to do more of them every single day.

I started spending more quality time with my friends and family, i started playing my favourite sport (Tennis) a few times a week, I chose to be grateful that I can even be alive on this earth, and I chose to be more loving and humble. Finally I also actively chose not to compare myself to people who were more "successful" than I was because comparing yourself to others can NEVER make you happy and will only make you feel inferior when you are not. Always remember that You are special, you are unique, and you are amazing.

After doing these things every single day, I had become a much happier person. It is all about perspective.

So what can you do to achieve happiness for yourself?

I recommend that you do the same thing I did which is to write down a list under the title "When Am I The Happiest?" or "When Was A Time When I Truly Felt Happy?" Start breaking down these memories as you recall your past, and down the essence of the memory. Everybody's list will be different as happiness means different things to every one of us. Once you have your answer, start doing more of these things everyday and tell me how you feel afterwards.

Some days you will forget about what makes you truly happy as you get bombarded by the harsh and cruel things life will throw at you. So I encourage you to put this list somewhere visible where you can see it everyday. Constantly remind yourself of what happiness means to you and shift your mind and body towards these actions every single day. I am sure you will be much happier person after that. See you in the next one :)

Chapter 4:
Happy People Have A Morning Ritual

For many of us, mornings begin in a rushed panic. We allow our alarm clocks to buzz at least a dozen times before deciding we have to get out of bed. Then we rush around our homes half-awake, trying to get ready for our day. In a hurry, we stub our toe on the bedpost, forget to put on deodorant, and don't pack a lunch because we simply don't have time. It's no wonder that so many folks despise the thought of being awake before 9 a.m.!

So it may not surprise you to know that the happiest and healthiest people tend to enjoy their mornings. They appear to thrive on waking up with the sun and look forward to a new day of possibilities. These people have humble morning rituals that increase their sense of well-being and give their day purpose.

Here are 3 morning habits that healthy and happy people tend to share:

1. They wake up with a sense of gratitude

Practicing gratitude is associated with a sense of overall happiness and a better mood—so it makes sense that the happiest and healthiest people we know start the day with a gratitude practice. This means that they're truly appreciative of their life and all of its little treasures. They practice small acts of gratitude in the morning by expressing thankfulness to their partner each morning before they rise from bed. They may also write about their gratefulness for five minutes each morning in a journal that they keep by their bedside.

2. **They begin every morning anew.**

The happiest and healthiest people know that every day is a brand-new day—a chance to start over and do something different. Yesterday may have been a complete failure for them, but today is a new day for success and adventure. Individuals who aren't ruined by one bad day are resilient creatures. Resiliency is a telltale sign of having purpose and happiness.

3. **They take part in affirmation, meditation, or prayer.**

Many of the happiest folks alive are spiritual. Affirmations are a way of reminding ourselves of all that we have going for us, and they allow us to engrain in our minds the kind of person we wish to be. Meditation helps keep our mind focused, calms our nerves, and supports inner peace. If you're already spiritual, prayer is a great way to connect and give thanks for whatever higher power you believe in.

Chapter 5:

Take Ownership of Yourself

What belongs to you but is used by other people more than you?

Your name.

And that's okay. People can use your name. But you must never allow yourself to lose ownership of you. In fact, you need to be incredibly conscious of taking ownership of everything that you are. And I do mean everything. Those few extra pounds, the nose you think is too big, your ginger hair or freckled skin. Whatever it is that you are insecure about, it's time that you showed up and took ownership. Because the moment you do your world will change.

But what does that look like? Why does it matter?

If someone parks a limo in the road outside your house, hands you the keys and tells you it is yours, what would you do? You're not just gonna put the keys in the ignition and leave it in the road. You are going to put that thing in a garage and get it insured. You will make sure that it is in a place where it is safe from weather and your jealous neighbour. Those are the things that you do when you take ownership of something. You make sure that they are protected because you value them. Then when you drive around town you don't look around as if you've stolen the thing. You drive with style and confidence. You are bold and comfortable because it belongs to you. *That* is what ownership looks like.

Now I know what you're thinking. That's easy to do with a limo, but I what I have is the equivalent of a car built before world war two. But the beautiful thing about ownership is that it does not depend on the object. It is not the thing being owned that you have to worry about, all you have to do is claim it. You've seen teenagers when they get their first car. Even if it is an old rust-bucket they drive around beaming with pride. Why? Because they know that what they have is theirs. It belongs to them and so they take ownership of it.

You have to do the same. You must take ownership of every part of you because in doing so you will keep it secure. You no longer have to be insecure about your weight if you know that that is where you are at right now. That doesn't mean you don't work for change though. It doesn't give you an excuse for stagnancy. You take accountability for your change and growth as much as you do for your present state. But in taking ownership you work towards polishing your pride, not getting rid of your low self-esteem. The difference may sound semantic, but the implications are enormous. The one allows you to work towards something and get somewhere good. The other makes it feel like you are just running away from something. And when you are running away then the only direction that matters is away – even if that means you run in circles.

Make a change today. Own yourself once more and be amazed at the rush that comes with it. With ownership comes confidence.

Chapter 6:
How To Find Your Passion

Today we're going to talk about a topic that i think many of you are interested to know about. And that is how to find your passion.

For many of us, the realities of work and obligations means that we end up doing something we dislike for the money in the hopes that it might buy us some happiness. That sometimes we stop following our passion because maybe it does not exactly pay very well. And that is a fair decision to make.

But today, i hope to be able to help you follow at least one passion project at any point in your life in the hopes that it might help elevate your spirits, give your life more meaning, and help you live each day with a renewed drive and purpose.

You see, the world can be very dull if we chase something that we actually don't really feel attracted to. For example, when we are forced to do something out of sheer dread day in and day out, it will suck the living soul out of us and we will tend to fall into the trap of running an endless wheel with no hope in sight. When we chase material things for example, money or luxury products, we sell our soul to a job that pays well physically but not emotionally and spiritually. As a human being, we have traded our very essence and time, for a piece of paper or digital currency that serves no purpose than to enrich us externally. While it might feel good to be living comfortably, past a certain threshold, there is a point of diminishing returns. And more money just doesn't bring you that much joy anymore.

Yes you may have the fanciest, car, house, and whatever physical possessions you have. But how many of you have heard stories of people who have a lot of money but end up depressed, or end up blowing it all away because they can never spend enough to satisfy their cravings for physical goods and services. What these people lacked in emotional growth, they tried to overcompensate with money. And as their inner self gets emptier and emptier, they themselves get poorer and poorer as well.

On the flip side, many would argue that passion is overrated. That passion is nothing but some imaginary thing that we tell ourselves we need to have in order to be happy. But i am here to argue that you do not need to make passion your career in order to be happy.

You see, passion is an aspiration, passion is something that excites you, passion is something that you would do even if it does not pay a single cent. That you would gladly trade your time readily for even if it meant u weren't getting anything monetary in return. Because this passion unlocks something within you that cannot be explained with being awarded physical prizes. It is the feeling that you are truly alive and happy, you are so incredibly grateful and thankful to be doing at that very moment in time, that nothing else mattered, not even sleep.

To me, and I hope you will see this too, that passion can be anything you make it out to be. It can be something as simple as a passion for singing, a passion for creating music, a passion for helping others, passion for supporting your family, passion for starting a family, passion for doing charity work, passion for supporting a cause monetarily, or even a passion for living life to the fullest and being grateful each day.

For some lucky ones, they have managed to marry their passion with their career. They have somehow made their favourite thing to do their job, and it fulfills them each day. To those people, i congratulate you and envy you.

But for the rest of us, our passion can be something we align our soul with as long as it fulfils us as well. If we have multiple mouths to feed, we can make our passion as being the breadwinner to provide for our family if it brings us joy to see them happy. If we have a day job that we hate but can't let go off for whatever reasons, we can have a passion for helping others, to use the income that we make to better the lives of others.

And for those who have free time but are not sure what to do with it, to just simply start exploring different interests and see what hobbies you resonate with. You may never know what you might discover if you did a little digging.

What I have come to realize is that passions rarely stay the same. They change as we change, they evolve over time just as we grow. And many of the passions we had when we were younger, we might outgrow them when we hit a certain age. As our priorities in life change, our passions follow along.

In my opinion, you do not need to make your passion your career in order to be truly happy.. I believe that all you need is to have at least 1 passion project at any given point of time in your life to sustain you emotionally and spiritually. Something that you can look forward to on your off days, in your time away from work, that you can pour all your time and energy into willingly without feeling that you have wasted any second. And who knows, you might feel so strongly about that passion project that you might even decide to make it your career some day. The thing is you never really know. Life is mysterious like that.

All I do know is that chasing money for the wrong reasons will never net u happiness. But having a passion, whatever it may be, will keep you grounded and alive.

So I challenge each and everyone of you today to look into your current life, and see there are any bright spots that you have neglected that you could revive and make it your passion project. Remember that passion can be anything you make out to be as long as you derive fulfilment and happiness from it. Helpfully one that isnt material or monetary.

Chapter 7:
6 Ways to Start All Over Again

If anyone tells you that you're meant to go from the crib to the running track, breeze through college, get your dream job, score the perfect partner, and live happily ever after all in one fell swoop, they're lying…and seriously delusional.

The reality is that life is anything but a straight line and is made up of seasons — some good, some mundane, and some so bad that you'll need plenty of time to recover from the trauma of living through it.

At your lowest point, you may think that your life is ruined and there's no way out.

But *listen* to me: **It WILL pass.** There's *always* a way forward. You just have to look for it. You can let the circumstances you're in ruin you, or you can allow it to improve you.

The process of rebuilding your life from the ground up won't be easy, but having a plan will greatly increase your chances of successfully carving out the life you want.

Here are my tried-and-tested steps to start with:

1. Start With Cleaning Up the Space You Live In

To build something good, you'll need good daily habits.

But to turn a new, unfamiliar (and therefore uncomfortable and 'quit-able') action into a daily habit, you'll need to do everything you can to reduce the odds that you'll give up, particularly when you hit a speed bump.

One of the best ways to do this is to set up your environment for your success.

This means clearing the space where you spend the most time of clutter, trash, and chaos.

The result: A calmer, clearer, and focused mind that'll help you move forward with your plan and sticking to it.

2. Make Peace With Reality and Work With, Not Against It

We often get stuck in life because we're either unable or unwilling to accept our reality as it is. Instead, we stubbornly continue to indulge in fantasy, specifically, how we wish things were.

This is where you'll need to get real with yourself, no matter how unpleasant it is.

Ask yourself: What's your situation now, and how can you work with what is, not what you wish it was?

3. Reflect On What and Where You Went Wrong

No one starts out planning to fail or creating a disaster.

But somehow, we end up taking one or several wrong steps along the way and find ourselves on a painful path we never expected to be in.

Whether these missteps were driven by ego, a lack of awareness, miscalculation, denial, or simply carelessness, you owe it to yourself, to be honest with the captain of your ship: You.

It's only once you've taken the time to reflect and figure out what went wrong and where things started to fall apart that you can start putting together a new plan with your success-driving strategy baked in.

This is the plan that'll help you make the progress you've wanted all along.

4. Revisit Your Goals and Values

But wait.

Before you take one step forward on your new path, you'll need to make sure your foundation is solid.

You may have an idea of where you'd like to go: Run it through a stress test:

How do you want to live?

Does your idea align with your values?

What are your values anyway?

What will you do if someone close to you disagrees or tries to tear it down?

What will happen if you find yourself feeling tempted to stray away from it?

Put your ideas, values, and stress-test answers down on paper so you can see them all in one place and let them sink in.

5. Decide what you Want To Do Next

Now that you've some ideas for possible paths you could take that fall in line with your values, it's time to decide: Which one will you choose?
'Decision' comes from the Latin word decision, which means "to cut off."
But while picking one path means cutting yourself off from all others, it doesn't mean that you can't course-correct later on by choosing a different one if things don't work out or feel right.

6. Work Up The Courage To Do It

It's OK to feel terrified about heading into new, unchartered territory. It'd be weird if you didn't. But know that this is the point where you start putting one foot in front of the other regardless of how you feel or chicken out and retreat into your cave. It's time to get moving despite the paralyzing fear and soul-crushing doubt that are making your feet and heart feel like lead.

Chapter 8:

10 Habits For A Clean Home

A clean home can make the homeowner a lot happier, less stressed, and even calmer. Waking up or coming back to a clutter-free and organized home can instantly brighten our mornings or even lift up our moods. But the thought of having to clean it extensively on weekends, for long hours, only to find the space in an absolute mess by midweek is like a nightmare and crestfallen.

Trust me when I say it is not that difficult maintaining a clean home. You need not necessarily have to deep clean your house almost every weekend for hours if you incorporate few very habits in your everyday routines. Today, we are exactly going to talk on this topic and hope to enlighten you to create a clean space.

Here are ten habits for a clean and happy home:

1. Make Your Bed As Soon as You Wake Up

We have heard a million times that the first thing that we should do after waking up is to make our beds, but how many of us incorporate this habit daily? An unmade bed can pull down the overall appearance of your bedroom by making it look messy. So take few moments and tuck those sheets and put your pillows in order. Change your bed sheets or duvet covers, and pillow covers as and when necessary.

Making our beds clean our most comfortable and visible area in the house and gives a sense of achievement helps us stay motivated and in a fresh state of mind throughout the day. If tucking in bed sheets daily is too annoying for you simply switch to duvet covers; that might save you from some hassle.

2. **Put Things Back in Place After Using Them**

Almost every home has this one chair or one spot that is cluttered with clothes and random knick-knacks, and this area hardly gets cleaned. Moreover, it is a normal human tendency to go on to dump more and more pieces of stuff and increase the pile size.

The idea behind creating this pile is that you will put away all the things in one go in a single day, but who are we kidding? As the pile starts increasing, we start pushing away the task of keeping the things back in their original place. The best way to avoid creating clutter is to put things back in their true place as soon as their job is done.

I completely understand that after finishing a task, we never feel like getting up to put them back in their home and hinder the task until we feel like doing so. But if you can consciously put this little effort into not letting things sit on the ground or in random places and put them back as soon as their job is done for the day, it is going to save a lot of time and help you have a clean space.

This is also applicable to your freshly washed clothes. As soon as you have them cleaned, fold them and put them in the drawer where it belongs. This will save you the headache of doing so on a Saturday morning which can then be used for reading your favorite book.

3. Take Your Mess With You as You Leave the Room

This is another essential practice that can bring a huge difference in your life and your home if turned into a habit. The idea here is to try not to leave a room empty-handed. What does this mean?

Let us take an example to understand this. Suppose you are in your living room and are going to the kitchen to drink water. Before you leave the living room, scan the room and look if any dirty bowl or plate is sitting in the room that needs to go to the kitchen. Take that cutlery along with you and keep them in the sink or dishwasher.

After making this a habit, you can then start following the one-touch rule that states that you touch a used item only once! That means if you are taking out the trash, make sure to dump or dispose of it properly and not just take it out and keep it somewhere on the porch or garden as this will kill the whole idea behind the habit. If you are moving something, it is better that you keep them where they belong, else, leave them be.

4. Have a House Cleaning Schedule

Maintain cleaning schedules like morning cleaning routines or weekly cleaning routines. This is basically distributing the cleaning of the entire house over an entire week rather than keeping the task to get done in a single day. Fix days for achieving a particular task, like on Wednesdays you can vacuum the living room and the bedroom and on Thursdays clean the other rooms and so on.

Make sure to assign 15 to 20 minutes each morning that you will strictly use for cleaning purposes. This will surely bring about a very positive impact on your house, and you will be in awe of how much cleaning can be done in those mere 15 - 20 minutes. Try to vacuum the hallways, entries, and all other high traffic regions of your home (including the kitchen) as frequently as possible as they tend to get dusty easily.

5. Maintain a Laundry Routine

Maintain a proper laundry routine depending on whether you live alone or in a family. As the pile of clothes grows enough to go into the washing, do the needful immediately. Do not delay the task endlessly as remember it is always easier to wash one load of clothing at a day rather than washing multiple loads of cloth in a day.

If you live with a family, do laundry every alternate day and if you live alone, then make sure to do your laundry every weekend. Also, make it a habit of putting the dirty clothes in the basket immediately after changing out of it rather than keeping them at random places to wash them later.

6. **Keep Your Shoes, Coats, and Umbrellas in Their Right Place**

Make it a habit to open your shoes near the entrance, put them away properly, and not randomly throw them. Keep a basket near the entryway where you can store all the umbrellas. If possible, put up a key holder on the door to keep the car keys and door keys in an organized manner.

•

The same goes for your long coats. Do not just dump them anywhere right after returning home! Have hooks hidden behind the entry door or have a sleek cupboard near the exit to store the trenchcoats and the long coats away from sight. These little changes will instantly clean up space.

7. **Relax Only After Finishing Your Chores**

If you have a chore that requires immediate attention, do it! Do not sit and relax, as this will go on to delay the chore indefinitely, and you may even forget to do it. So get your chores done first, then sit and watch Netflix. Detain your tasks only when you are exhausted and desperately need a break.

8. **Clean After Every Meal**

Right after fishing your meal, clean up the place. I know what most of you are thinking, but trust me, relaxing after cleaning everything up will give you more satisfaction and help you have a cleaner home for sure. After having your lunch or dinner, keep all the plates in the washer and make sure to also clean the utensils that you used for cooking.

Clean the countertops, the burners, and also the table that you sat and ate on. Cleaning the countertops and tables immediately will save your furniture from an ugly stain and help you save a lot of energy and time you might have had to put in if you try to clean the spill the later day.

9. Clean Your Dishes and Sink Every Night

I wanted to say have a nighttime cleaning routine every day where you clean all the dishes from dinner or any other remaining dishes of the day, the sink, and the kitchen by placing all the ingredient containers in their rightful places. The nighttime routine would also include setting your dining table, setting the cushions on your sofa, and clearing out your fridge so that you have a clean and spacious fridge before you unpack your groceries.

But I understand that not many of us have the energy after a hectic day at work, so instead of doing the entire routine, just make sure to wash all the dishes and clean the sink thoroughly so that you wake up to a beautiful kitchen in the morning. I mean, who wants to wake up to a pile of dishes, right? Just give some extra time at night to clean out the kitchen to have a fresh start in the morning.

10. Get Rid Of Unnecessary Things

To have a clutter-free space, each item in your home must have a home of its own. For example, if you do not have a place to hang your towels, they will likely be lying here and there and making the space look messy. Thus, make sure each item has its own place to sleep. If you see there are free-flowing items, then it is time to declutter!

You do not need much space, but you definitely need fewer items that fit in the available space and are easier to manage. More items require more time to clean and put things away properly. Thus, it is easier and requires less time to clean a room with lesser items out on the floor or on the countertop. Hence, make it a habit of getting rid of all the unnecessary items. You can donate the items or gift them to your neighbors or friends. Recycle all the old newspaper and magazines as papers too contribute a lot to the messiness of any room.

Extra Tip: Always try to keep your cleaning supplies in easily visible and accessible areas. This will save you a lot of time and motivate you to clean up anything that should be done as soon as possible.

Be satisfied with clean enough! A home can neither be squeaky clean every day nor can it be cleaned in one day. It is a gradual process that requires a conscious effort being made daily.

A clean home can be easily achieved by following these tips and manifesting these practices as your daily habits.

Chapter 9: Happy People Savor the Moment

Learning to "savor the moment" in life is a convenient, free, and effective way to increase your happiness and quality of life and reduce stress. Enjoying what you have can help you to appreciate what you've got rather than lamenting what you don't have and creating stress by striving for too much. Being able to savor the moment with loved ones can bring a stronger connection and sense of appreciation, which leads to better quality relationships and all the benefits of social support that they bring. Learn more about these techniques to savor the moment in life.

1. Focus on Details

Sometimes as we go through life, we forget to stop and enjoy the little things; indeed, it's possible to go through an entire day either stuck in your ruminations about the past or anxious over the future, never really seizing the moment and noticing the pleasant things that are happening right now (and passing up positive opportunities right and left). As you savor the moment, notice the little things that can make a day special — the smile of a friend, the kindness of a stranger, the beauty of a sunset

2. **Focus on Sensations**

As you're experiencing your day, notice and memorize the details — especially the positive details — of what's happening around you. Create a memory. Notice the sounds you hear, like the sound of children's laughter in the background. Notice the smells, like the scent of a fresh sea breeze. And how did that wind feel on your face? Noticing these types of sensory details helps you live fully in the moment and can help evoke pleasant memories when you hear music, smell aroma, or feel sensations you experience on the days you want to savor.

3. **Focus on the Positive**

As humans, we're naturally wired to notice the negative events in life more than the positive, as these are what we need to keep track of to maintain our safety: if we're aware of threats around us, we're more able to launch a defense. However, if we actively focus on the positive, we can stress less and enjoy life more from an increasingly optimistic vantage point. To savor the moment, notice what's going right, and appreciate it. This isn't the same as pretending you're happy when you're not; it's more about noticing the things that lead to greater happiness and reduced stress.

4. **Express Gratitude**

Feeling gratitude goes along with noticing the positive and is an excellent way to savor the moment. Notice all the nice things that people do for you (and thank them whenever possible), or simply notice what you enjoy about people when they're just themselves (and be sure to tell them that, too). Appreciate what goes right in your day as it happens, and write it down in a gratitude journal at night — it's a surprisingly effective way to both raise your level of daily gratitude and build a record of all the things in your life that can make you happy when you're having a bad day.

Chapter 10: Happy People Create Time to Do What They Love Every Day

Most of our days are filled with things that we need to do and the things we do to destress ourselves. But, in between all this, we never get time for things. We wanted to do things that bring us pure joy. So then the question is, When will we find time to do what we love? Then, when things calm down a bit and when the people who visit us leave or finish all the trips we have planned and wrap up our busy projects, and the kids will be grown, we will retire? Then, probably after we are dead, we will have more time.

You do not have to wait for things to get less busy or calmer. There will always be something coming up; trips, chores, visitors, errands, holidays, projects, death and illness. There is never going to be more time. Whatever you have been stuck in the past few years, it will always be like that. So now the challenge is not waiting for things to change it is to make time for things you love no matter how busy your life is. Sit down and think about what you want to do, something that you have been putting off. What is something that makes you feel fulfilled and happy? Everyone has those few things that make them fall in love with life think of what is that for you. If you haven't figured it out yet, we will give you some examples, and maybe you can try some of these things and see how that makes you feel.

- Communing with nature
- Going for a beautiful walk
- Creating or growing a business or an organization
- Hiking, running, biking, rowing, climbing
- Meditating, journaling, doing yoga, reflecting
- Communing with loved ones
- Crafting, hogging, blogging, logging, vlogging
- Reading aloud to kids
- Reading aloud to kids

Did you remember something you enjoyed doing, but as the responsibilities kept increasing, you sidelined it. Well, this is your sign to start doing what you loved to take time out for that activity every day, even if it is for 30 minutes only. Carve that time out for yourself, do it now. Once you start doing this, you will realize that you will have more energy because your brain will release serotonin, and your energy level will increase. Secondly, your confidence will improve because you will be making something love every day, and that will constantly help you gain confidence because you will be putting yourself in a happy, self-loving state. You will notice that you have started enjoying life more when you do something you love once a day. It makes the rest of your day brighter and happier. You will also want to constantly continue learning and growing because your brain will strive to do more and more of the thing you like to do, and that will eventually lead to an increased desire of learning and growing. Lastly, your motivation will soar because you will have something to look forward to that brings you pure joy.

Chapter 11:

Ten Habits You Must Stop If You Want To Manifest What You Want In Life

We all have our deep secret desires of what we would want to turn into buried in our hearts. We hardly say it aloud lest we are judged harshly by an ungrateful society. It is ungrateful because the same society that celebrates when you in your win shall bash you when you slip.

You may have tried out very many things to bring to life your not-so-alive wishes but your efforts have been in vain. Here are ten things that you must stop if you want to manifest what you want in life:

1. Trusting Everhbody

You may have heard of an old saying that you should keep your friends close and your enemies even closer. This is true especially when you are about to make a major move. Open trust is often violated and you will suffer a series of heartbreaks if you do not cease handing people your trust on a platter.

Trust is earned. Let your friends earn it by continuously proving their loyalty and friendship to you. If you give the wrong people your trust, they will stand in your way of manifesting what you want in life. They will poison your dreams and before you know it, you have lost it all.

2. Sharing yYour Plans Openly

It is not everybody who has your best interest at heart. Some people close to you could be orchestrating your downfall and the more information you reveal the easier it is to bring you down. Be unpredictable if you want to manifest what you want in life.

Manifestation requires some degree of secrecy. Work in silence and let your success introduce you. Stop being an open book for others to read. What could be an innocent act of honesty can turn the tables against you and hinder manifestation.

3. <u>Procrastination</u>

To procrastinate is to postpone action to a later time without proper reason. Sometimes an idea would strike your mind and instead of implementing it immediately, you decide to wait to act after some time. This will make you lose sight of what you wanted to do.

Procrastination kills unborn dreams and is an enemy to your progress. Strike the rod when it is hot. You can consult with people you trust before taking a concrete decision after which you must not delay implementing it.

4. <u>Taking Issues Lightly</u>

There is a big problem when you consider everything at face value. There is always more than what meets the eye. Stop assuming what people say on something concerning you and investigate their motive. This is how you will sift genuine friends from fake ones.

Question the obvious if you have any doubt. This will make you have clarity of mind to make sober decisions. Manifestation requires sobriety. What you overlook or assume could make a great difference in decision-making.

5. Blaming Other People

Great people do not play the blame game. Instead, they innovate solutions to existing problems. They are proactive in society and this makes them stand out in a highly polarized environment.

Stop blaming people for your woes, real or perceived, and work towards not falling into the same trap again. Excuses stand in the way of the manifestation of your dreams. Do not cry foul every time things go wrong. Choose to make them right and chart your way forward. Two wrongs do not make a right.

6. Allowing Other People To Make Deciison On Your Behalf

Why should someone else make decisions for you while you are not incapacitated? They could be biased to your dreams and make key decisions out of line with your goals. Stop giving them the mandate to run your life, do it yourself.

It is right to accept advice and heed it but it does not mean that your advisors should make decisions for you. You choose whether or not to heed the advice. The ultimate responsibility of decision-making rests with you.

7. Casting aspersions On Your Ability

You should not doubt your ability or competence; when you do, nobody will believe you. Self-doubt gives other people the license to demean and underestimate your ability. Manifestation requires self-confidence on your part.

In his book, *the 48 laws of power,* Robert Greene writes that you should enter action with boldness. Conversely, you sign your death warranty when you timidly shy away from challenges thrown your way.

8. Disrespecting Authority

Rebellion to authorities is a sign of weakness and bad character. Respect authority from the family to the national level because they are in place to bring equality and level the playing field for its people from all races and backgrounds.

How can you expect manifestation for what you want in life when you are rebellious to the same authority supposed to take care of you? You will similarly be disrespected when you are in a position of power.

9. Being Pessimistic

Pessimism has closed potential doors of breakthrough for many people. It crushes any hope of success left. To succeed in what you do, you need to take the initiative despite the odds being against you. You will not see anything good when you are pessimistic.

A pessimistic mind is an enemy of progress. It makes you your own worst enemy. Remove this barrier and start thinking positively and you will make great gains in life.

10. Making A Comparison Of Your Life With Others

Life does not come with a manual. Everybody has their question paper to tackle. You therefore cannot copy from anyone else. It is disastrous when you copy the lifestyle of somebody else. You lose your identity when you judge yourself by another person's standards.

Your success is different from your neighbors'. Be encouraged when you clap for other people until your turn arrives. Stop judging yourself harshly if you have not won like your neighbor. Celebrate with them as you count the blessings at your doorstep.

In conclusion, it is agreeable that there are bad habits we ought to stop if we want to manifest what we want in life. These ten habits shed light on a dozen others that we need to stop to achieve manifestation.

Chapter 12:

How Much Is Your Time Really Worth?

What is the biggest mistake we make in life? Perhaps Buddha's most suitable answer was given by "The biggest mistake is you think you have time." While our time in this world is free, it's also priceless. We can neither own it nor keep it, but we can use it and spend it. And once it's all lost, it's inevitable that we will never get it back.

"Your time is limited, so don't waste it living someone else's life." - Steve Jobs. Our time is limited in this world is both good and bad news. The bad news is that time flies and never returns, but the good news is that we're the pilot. The average person lives 78 years on this planet. We spend almost one-third of our lives sleeping; that's approximately 28.3 years from our lives. And still, 30% of us struggle to sleep well. We spend almost 10.5 years of our life working, but over 50% of us want to leave our current jobs. Time is a valuable asset, even more so than money. We can get more money, but we can never get more time.

After all of the years we spend doing chores, shopping, grooming, eating, drinking, TV, and social media, time leaves us with only nine years. Now the question arises, how will we spend that time? Just like we would never waste our money on something gratuitous, why do we waste our time on it? We might think that people are wasting our time when we are the ones permitting them to do that in reality. We sometimes end up losing our most beloved people because we don't value their time. Some of us don't recognize their importance until they're gone.

Every day, from the moment we wake up till the moment we get back to sleep, two voices are battling inside our heads; one wants to uplift us and one that holds us back. And which one will win? The one that we listen to the most. The one that we feed us the most. The one that we amplify. Similarly, it's up to us and our choice how we use that time in our hands. William Shakespeare once said, "Time is prolonged for those who want, very fast for those who are scared, very long for those who are sad, and very short for those who celebrate, but for those who love, time is eternal." We should make the most out of our time and learn its value by carefully analyzing what life teaches us about it.

Chapter 13:
The Only Obstacle Is Yourself

Ever wondered why you feel low all the time?

Why it seems like everyone is better than you?

Why everyone excels at something that you wished you were good at too?

I am sure you have wondered about at least one of these at one or another instance in your life.

These questions remain unanswered no matter how hard you try. Until you realize that the only answer that fits the puzzle is that, it is because of you.

All these barriers and limitations are placed upon you not because you are stupid or incapable.

It is merely because you have limiting beliefs about yourself that stop you from achieving your fullest potential.

It is because you are not trying hard enough to make yourself stand apart from everyone else in the world.

If you lag at school, study hard.

If your lag at your job, socialize more.

If you are obese, break a sweat to lose all that fat.

If you lack some technical skill, learn till you beat the very best in that field.

Don't blame others for your failures.

Everyone else starts off with the same resources and expertise as you.

If others can succeed, Why can't you?

Who is stopping you from flying high in victory?

If no one else tells you, let me do the honors; it's you.

You are the biggest cause of everything that is happening in your life right now.

Nothing is good or bad unless you do or don't do something to generate that result.

Make a promise to yourself today that you will achieve something great by the end of this week.

Envision the big picture and start watching yourself get drawn into that picture.

Take baby steps. take a big leap of faith.

Move one foot forward over the other no matter how big or small.

Once you get past the fear of being stuck where you currently are,

life will start opening great doors to your every step forward.

Sometimes we may take a step back.

Sometimes life throws us durians instead of lemons.

As long as you dust yourself off and move again you are never going to lose.

Don't idealize someone if you are not ready to idealize yourself.

To envision yourself charting your own path, in your own unique pair of shoes.

If for whatever reason you don't achieve that something someday, don't beat yourself up for it.

Maybe those shoes weren't the right fit for you.

Try another pair of shoes, and walk down a new path with confidence.

This could be a blessing in disguise for you.

A lesson for you to strive towards something new.

Something better. Something that no one has ever dreamed of or done before.

If along the way some someone comes and tells you to stop, and you stop to hear them say that to you, it wasn't their fault, but yours. Because you were idle enough to be distracted by others to compromise that dream.

Don't lift your head until you have achieved something today. Don't say a word to anyone about your goals.

Spend more and more time to figure out your life. Promise yourself that no one else matters in your life till you have achieved everything and you are left with nothing more to achieve.

I remember the time my father told me to be a better man than him. The time when I fell off my bicycle for the first time. He came to me and said, 'Don't give up now, as you will fall every day, but when you rise you will achieve bigger and better things than you could ever wish'.

My father gave me his hand when I needed it the most and he still does. But when he is gone and there is no one free enough or caring enough left to see me go through all that struggle, then I will be the closest figure to my father to back me up and give me the courage to get up and start again till I succeed in riding the bike of life.

You and I are capable of riding the high tide. Either we ride it all the way to the shore or we drown to never get back up again. It's up to us now what we want to do. It's you who decides what you were and what you can be!

You will regret yourself the most when you finally come to realize that it was 'You' who brought you down. So don't waste yourself and make a vow today, a vow to be the best you can be and the rest will be history.

Chapter 14:

Reach Peak Motivation

Remember the time when you wanted a sign, a person, a comment, an event, just anything that could maybe make you realize once again that everything is happening for real and that you actually have a presence? Remember the feeling?

I am sure we all had those times. And we often still have and maybe have some more to come. But the question is a big mystery that everyone goes through with a rough answer alongside it.

We all have a vague idea somewhere in our heads. We all have some idea somewhere wandering within us but we cease t find it with all our efforts going in vain. There is this struggle with the world that we keep fighting and then there is this quest that we always seem to be on, where we keep looking for answers.

Let me give you some tips for that. You are looking for motivation within yourself because you think the world can't do one for you. It is true to most extent, but the world is not your servant. Nature still gives you things to be proud of and be inspired from. But we keep neglecting the signs of nature.

Situations often present themselves as if we are not meant to be where we are right now. It may be true. But then the world starts to push you down, you will always find reasons at the bottom from where you would want to take a new step forward!

You will always find new ways to become motivated and inspired. Because you need to be dead to become hopeless and motionless, not wanting to do one more thing that could contribute towards a better life.

Till the day you are alive, it's a sin for you to feel hopeless and without purpose.

The fear of failure is always real. But the fear of not being able to feel content and happy once you reach the top is not a reason to not look or stop looking for newer and better things.

Life has endless possibilities and not all have to be bad always. You will get bigger and better chances more than often. But you have to remain motivated enough to avail them for better once they finally present themselves.

You don't have to be bad to fail at something. Even the best of the best fail and they fail more than a regular person. But that doesn't give them a reason to stop rather they get more motivated and energetic to stick to the cause and for what they believe in.

If one thing is important enough and you believe in it enough you will always stay connected to that thing someway or somehow.

But for that, you have to believe in your abilities. That no matter what happens, if you stay committed enough, there is no way in heaven or hell that can keep you away from success and the things that you most want in your life.

Every mountain is within reach if you keep going and keep believing that you are one more step close to the summit.

Chapter 15:
How To Have The Best Day Everyday

We all have the power to create the kind of day we want to experience every time we go to sleep and wake up the next day.

It is normal to think that we will only have an amazing day when something good happens to us. We believe that good things only happen out of luck, chance, fate, or whatever, but we never think that we can create a good day just by our sheer desire to.

What the best day means to each of us may be different, some prioritise professional accomplishments as their measurement of a great day, some prioritise spending time with as many friends as possibly in a 24 hour period as one that is great. But when we depend on these circumstances, we are never really in full control of our day because bad things can always happen without a rhyme or reason. Our presentation that we have been working months on could suddenly be marred by a technical difficulty, or our friends could cancel on us last minute due to whatever reason.

What we thought would be our best day could turn out to be one filled with disappointments and maybe even loneliness.

I struggle with this all the time. Everytime i had built up the perfect day in my head, something always seem to go wrong somehow and I am left searching for a filler to cover that void. Through the fault of nobody but life getting the way, as it always does, I found out that if I always depended on others to give me the best day, that it rarely ever happens. Occasionally things work out great when I least expect it, but those occurrences are still out of my control.

It is only when we decide for ourselves that we can have the best day regardless of life inserting itself in, that we can truly enjoy every waking moment of our lives. By constantly reminding ourselves that we are grateful to be alive, to live each moment in the present, and to live as though tomorrow might never come, we can truly appreciate the little things in life that we often overlook. We have the best day because we believe that it is.

From the moment that we get out of bed, we appreciate the first breath we take, the first shower that we take, the first meal that we take, and all the little things that make up our wonderful day. Appreciating the fact that we are living with a roof over our heads, that we have clean water to drink, air conditioning to keep us cool, heaters to keep us warm, literally anything and everything around us, there is something to be grateful for.

When we start to notice that our life is truly amazing, we will never have to depend on other things or other people to make us have our best day. That is the kind of control we have over our day if we set it off on the right foot from the get-go.

It was only when I started being grateful for the fact that I am truly blessed with an amazing family, pet, friends, a house, that I realized i didn't need fancy party or fancy things to allow me to have the best day ever. Yes there are moments in life when we feel truly alive, those moments we will cherish and remember, but those moments are also few and far between. If we can take control of the other 364 days of the year, we would truly be the happiest people alive on this earth who are living their best days everyday.

Chapter 16:

10 Habits That Give Me Joy

Joy is an innate feeling of extreme happiness that one experiences. It bubbles within your spirit before it manifests physically for others to see. Unlike happiness, joy is not easily put off because it is brought by your actions without external influence. Do acts that will satisfy you and impact the people around you positively.

These are ten habits that will bring you joy:

1. Belief in God

Human beings feel the need to believe in a superior being. Almost everyone believes in the existence of a superior deity that sustains life. He is God. The relationship between God and man is like that of a parent and their children. Their presence in the lives of their children is very important because they provide for their needs and protect them from the harsh world.

When you believe in God, you will not have to worry about issues beyond your control because God will take care of you. He will guide you through life and lead you away from worldly sorrows. Your joy will be akin to that of a child who walks beside their parents. They have nothing to worry about.

2. Staying Debt-Free

Shackles of debt have tied people and nations to their debtors. They always look over their shoulders to see if someone is after them especially when it is time to service their debt. This denies you the joy of life in living as a free person.

Avoid entering into unnecessary debt regardless of how flexible the terms of service could be. Debt is attractive because it promises to solve your problems instantly. However, it only postpones the reality to some future date. You will have joy when you live your life within your means and not enter into debt to sustain your needs.

3. Living My Ideal Dream

Quite a handful of people live their ideal lives. While growing up we have a fantasy of the kind of life we would want to live, the nature of families we would want to have, and the type of work we want to do. Sometimes miss part of our dream package but still, life has to move on.

You live your ideal life when you fulfill any of your dreams in life because not everyone gets such a blessing. People are stuck in jobs they dread but cannot quit because they have to fend for themselves and their families. It is joyous to live life as you had envisaged.

4. Success In My Work

Our work and businesses are sources of income in our lives. They pay our bills and sustain our needs. Life is rough when business is not favorable. We would do everything possible to maintain our jobs or business because we rely on them.

We are joyous whenever we get promoted at work, or when our businesses flourish. Our mastery of skills could seal our opportunities. Whatever your specialty could be, perfect your skills at work and you will be successful. Success at work will bring you joy in life.

5. A Well-Knit Relationship With Family and Friends

We are social beings and are interdependent. No man is an island. At any point in our lives, we need the support of other people no matter how much we try to dissociate ourselves.

When you have a healthy relationship with your family and friends, you will unconsciously attract joy. How beautiful it is to have a shoulder to lean on during hard times! They will comfort and encourage you when your spirit is low. Cultivate a healthy relationship with them and you will live a joyful life.

6. Mentoring Someone

People will forget what you said but will never forget how you made them feel. Be careful how you present yourself to people and guard your reputation at all costs. You never know who could be watching.

There is joy when you mentor someone to walk into your steps and watch them grow. You can associate yourself with their success and achievements. It is a form of investment in a person that can never go bad. Your impact can be felt even in your absence. It is as if you are reincarnated.

7. Exploring The World

The world has diverse cultures and there is always something new to learn. Do not be tied to your locality because your thinking will be limited to only what you can see. Familiarity breeds contempt. When you stay at one place for long, people will get tired of you and take you for granted. They will overlook your presence and you will be depressed about it.

Traveling to new places brings the joy of a child because of new experiences. You will be happy to discover new things and exchange ideas with other people. The reason why children are always joyful is that they always find small things fascinating, unlike adults who are familiar with everything in their environment.

8. Adapting To Change

We cannot escape from change no matter how hard we try. It is impossible to live as you did a few years ago and ignore how much the world has changed. Those who live in denial are depressed because of their inability to adapt to change.

You will attract joy if you are flexible in life. Nobody has a monopoly of ideas on how to live life. Do not be rigid in what you know because you will be disappointed when it is no longer fashionable.

9. Be Content And Appreciative

Staying content is a rare trait to find in a world where people's ambitions have clouded their judgment, making them irrational. You will always be bitter if are not appreciative of what you have because there is always somebody who is one step ahead of you in life.

Being content does not stop you from being ambitious. Joy comes when you derive satisfaction from the simple things in life. Do not wait for greater things for you to be joyful. Joy comes in small packages that we often overlook.

10. Develop Hobbies

Hobbies are what we do to relax from our busy schedules. They are what we do apart from work. We can do them alone or with the company of other people. It could be swimming, singing, traveling, playing soccer, reading novels, or writing.

Hobbies attract joy because there is no pressure to perform and nobody to judge us. You can be yourself with no one to please but yourself.

In conclusion, there is a distinction between joy and happiness. Joy comes from within you while happiness is greatly influenced by other people in our lives. These ten habits bring me joy, so shall they to you if you consider them.

Chapter 17:
7 Ways To Remove Excess Noise In Your Life

Ever felt lost in a world that is so fast-paced, where no two moments are the same? Do you ever have a hard time achieving your goals, just because you have more distractions than a purpose to jump to success?

We live in a time, where technology is the biggest ease as well as the biggest difficulty while achieving our goals.

When you need something to be fixed, the internet can save us a lot of time, but the same internet can prove to be the biggest cause to take away the focus of the most determined too.

Although there are many important things on the internet too, that are essential to our daily lives, we don't need them at all times. Especially the realm of social media platforms.

Youtube, Facebook even Instagram can prove to be a beneficial tool for learning and teaching. But it can also make you spend more and more time on things that won't give you much except a good laugh here and there.

So what habits or activities can you adapt to distill these distractions. Reduce noise in life helping you focus better on the things that matter the most.

1. Divide your Tasks Into Smaller Ones

When you already have many distractions in life, including the household tasks and other daily life chores that you must attend to, then you must not avoid those.

But your dreams and goals must not be put aside at all, instead one must learn to complete them by dividing them into smaller, more manageable tasks.

Those who depend on you must have you when they need you, but that shouldn't stop you from doing what you require from yourself.

That can be done by keeping your head in the work whenever you get the chance to get maximum results from those short intervals.

2. Manage Your Time Smartly

Life is too short to be indulging in every whim and activity that you crave. Not everything or thought requires you to act upon.

A human being is the smartest being on this planet but also the stupidest. When a man or a woman wants to achieve something with all their heart, they do get it eventually. But when they have a thousand silly desires to go for, they slide off the set path as if there were none.

"You only Live Once".

Logically, this is a valid quote to get anyone off their path to success. But, realistically this is also the most common reason for the failure of a majority of our youngsters.

You only get this life once, So you must go for the acts that bring you a better future with a surety of freedom without having to rely on anyone. Life doesn't need to be a continuous struggle once you use your energies at the right time for the right time.

3. Get Your Head Out of Social Media

I know this may sound a little Grownup and cliched, but we spend more time on our mobiles and laptops than going out and doing something physically in all our senses with our actual hands.

We can believe and act on anything that pops up on this screen but rarely do we get anything worthwhile that we can adapt to change our lives once and for all.

Social media might be the new medium and source of knowledge and business for many, but for a layman, this is also the biggest waste of creative energy.

There is a lot out there to do in real life, a lot that we can realistically achieve. But, these days, we tend to hide behind a simple tweet and believe that we have done enough when the reality could have been much different.

4. Avoid Unhealthy Relationships

You might have always heard that a friend can be an emotional escape when you need one, but the excess of friends can prove to be the opposite of that. People seem to think, the more friends you have, the better you have a chance to stay engaged and have a happy social life. But this isn't always the case.

The more you have friends, your devotion gets scattered and you find solace in everyone's company. This makes you more exposed, and people might take advantage of that. The fewer friends you have, the better loyalty you can expect and better returns of a favor.

When you have fewer friends, even if you lose one someday or get deceived, you would require less time to bounce back from the incident and you won't have to worry for long.

5. Get Out of Home Environment

Productivity required a productive environment. People tend to look for ease, but it doesn't always help us with finding our true potential.

You sometimes need a strict office environment or a more organized station or workplace. A place where there is no distraction or source of wandering thoughts to get your attention.

People need to understand how our brains work. If you cannot focus sitting in your bed, get a chair and a table. If that doesn't work for you, take a stool without a backrest. If you still feel at ease, just pick a standing table and start working while standing on your feet.

This makes your mind stay more focused on the task at hand to be done quickly.

6. Make A Schedule For These Distractions

If you feel like you can't give up the urge to pick your phone and check your feed. Or if you need to watch the last quarter of the league, Or if you need to have a smoke.

Don't start fighting these urges. It won't help you, rather make things worse.

If you cannot let go off of these things, it's fine. Make a deal with your brain, that you need this last page done within the next 10 minutes, and then I can go do what I needed direly.

You have to come at peace with your mind and work as a single unit. So make time for these distractions and gradually you might be able to drop them once and for all.

7. You Don't Have to Compare With Anyone

Why do we humans need to compare and compete? Because we think it keeps our drive and our struggle alive. We think it gives us a reason and a purpose to go on and makes us see our goals more clearly.

Comparing to others won't make you see 'Your Goals', rather you would start creating goals that were never meant to be for you. You have these priorities just because you saw someone with something that appealed to you.

This is the noise and distraction that deviates you from the path that was meant to be for you all along.

If you want a clear vision of what you want, start removing cluttered thoughts, acts, and people from your life. It might seem hard at the start, but you won't have any regrets once everything comes in place.

Chapter 18:

How To Worry Less

How many of you worry about little things that affect the way you go about your day? That when you're out with your friends having a good time or just carrying out your daily activities, when out of nowhere a sudden burst of sadness enters your heart and mind and immediately you start to think about the worries and troubles you are facing. It is like you're fighting to stay positive and just enjoy your day but your mind just won't let you. It becomes a tug of war or a battle to see who wins?

How many of you also lose sleep because your mind starts racing at bedtime and you're flooded with sad feelings of uncertainty, despair, worthlessness or other negative emotions that when you wake up, that feeling of dread immediately overwhelms you and you just feel like life is too difficult and you just dont want to get out of bed.

Well If you have felt those things or are feeling those things right now, I want to tell you you're not alone. Because I too struggle with those feelings or emotions on a regular basis.

At the time of writing this, I was faced with many uncertainties in life. My business had just ran into some problems, my stocks weren't doing well, I had lost money, my bank account was telling me I wasn't good enough, but most importantly, i had lost confidence. I had lost the ability to face each day with confidence that things will get better. I felt that i was worthless and that bad things will always happen to me. I kept seeing the negative side of things and it took a great deal of emotional toll on me. It wasn't like i chose to think and feel these things, but they just came into my mind whenever they liked. It was like a parasite feeding off my negative energy and thriving on it, and weakening me at the same time.

Now your struggles may be different. You may have a totally different set of circumstances and struggles that you're facing, but the underlying issue is the same. We all go through times of despair, worry, frustration, and uncertainty. And it's totally normal and we shouldn't feel ashamed of it but to accept that it is a part of life and part of our reality.

But there are things we can do to minimise these worries and to shift to a healthier thought pattern that increases our ability to fight off these negative emotions.

I want to give you 5 actionable steps that you can take to worry less and be happier. And these steps are interlinked that can be carried out in fluid succession for the greatest benefit to you. But of course you can choose whichever ones speaks the most to you and it is more important that you are able to practice any one of these steps consistently rather than doing all 5 of them haphazardly. But I want to make sure I give you all the tools so that you can make the best decisions for yourself.

Try this with me right now as I go through these 5 steps and experience the benefit for yourself instead of waiting until something bad happens.

The very first step is simple. Just breathe. When a terrible feeling of sadness rushes into your body out of nowhere, take that as a cue to close your eyes, stop whatever you are doing, and take 5 deep breathes through your nose. Breathing into your chest and diaphragm. Deep breathing has the physiological benefit of calming your nerves and releasing tension in the body and it is a quick way to block out your negative thoughts. Pause the video if you need to do practice your deep breathing before we move on.

And as you deep breathe, begin the second step. Which is to practice gratefulness. Be grateful for what you already have instead of what you think u need to have to be happy. You could be grateful for your dog, your family, your friends, and whatever means the most to you. And if you cannot think of anything to be grateful for, just be grateful that you are even alive and walking on this earth today because that is special and amazing in its own right.

Next is to practice love and kindness to yourself. You are too special and too important to be so cruel to yourself. You deserve to be loved and you owe it to yourself to be kind and forgiving. Life is tough as it is, don't make it harder. If you don't believe in yourself, I believe in you and I believe in your worthiness as a person that you have a lot left to give.

The fourth step is to Live Everyday as if it were your last. Ask yourself, will you still want to spend your time worrying about things out of your control if it was your last day on earth? Will you be able to forgive yourself if you spent 23 out of the last 24 hours of your life worrying? Or will you choose to make the most out of the day by doing things that are meaningful and to practice love to your family, friends, and yourself?

Finally, I just want you to believe in yourself and Have hope that whatever actions you are taking now will bear fruition in the future. That they will not be in vain. That at the end of the day, you have done everything to the very best of your ability and you will have no regrets and you have left no stone unturned.

How do you feel now? Do you feel that it has helped at least a little or even a lot in shaping how you view things now? That you can shift your perspective and focus on the positives instead of the worries?

If it has worked for you today, I want to challenge you to consistently practice as many of these 5 steps throughout your daily lives every single day. When you feel a deep sadness coming over you, come back to this video if you need guidance, or practice these steps if you remember them on your own.

I wish you only good things and I hope that I have helped you that much more today. Thank you for your supporting me and this channel and if you find that I can do more for you, do subscribe to my channel and I'll see you in the next one. Take care.

Chapter 19:

Happy People Are Busy but Not Rushed

Dan Pink points to an interesting new research finding — the happiest people are those that are very busy but don't feel rushed:

Who among us are the happiest? Newly published research suggests that fortunate folks have little or no excess time and yet seldom feel rushed.

This clicks with me. I love blogging, but I hate being under time pressure to get it done. This tension is very nicely demonstrated in a recent study by Hsee et al. (2010). When given a choice, participants preferred to do nothing unless given the tiniest possible reason to do something: a piece of candy. Then they sprang into action.

Not only did people only need the smallest inducement to keep busy, but they were also happier when doing something rather than nothing. It's as if people understand that being busy will keep them happier, but they need an excuse of some kind.

Having plenty of time gives you a feeling of control. Anything that increases your *perception of control* over a situation (whether it increases your control or not) can substantially decrease your stress level.

In Colorado, Steve Maier at the University of Boulder says that the degree of control that organisms can exert over something that creates stress determines whether the stressor alters the organism's functioning. His findings indicate that only uncontrollable stressors cause harmful effects. Inescapable or uncontrollable stress can be destructive, whereas the same stress that feels escapable is less destructive, significantly so… **Over and over, scientists see that the perception of control over a stressor alters the stressor's impact.**

But heavy time pressure stresses you out and kills creativity. Low-to-moderate time pressure produces the best results.

If managers regularly set impossibly short time-frames or impossibly high workloads, employees become stressed, unhappy, and unmotivated—burned out. Yet, people hate being bored. It was rare for any participant in our study to report a day with very low time pressure, such days—when they did occur—were also not conducive to positive inner work life. In general, low-to-moderate time pressure seems optimal for sustaining positive thoughts, feelings, and drives.

Your reaction to being too busy and under time pressure might be to want to do nothing. But that can drop you into the bottom left corner. And this makes you more unhappy than anything:

…**surveys "continue to show the least happy group to be those who quite often have excess time." Boredom, it seems, is burdensome.**

So, stay busy—set goals. Challenge yourself, but make sure you have plenty of time to feel in control of the situation.

This is how games feel. And games are fun.

Chapter 20:
Enjoying The Simple Things

Today we're going to talk about a topic that might sound cheesy, but trust me it's worth taking a closer look at. And that is how we should strive to enjoy the simple things in life.

Many of us think we need a jam packed schedule for the week, month, or year, to tell us that we are leading a very productive and purposeful life. We find ways to fill our time with a hundred different activities. Going to this event, that event, never slowing down. And we find ourselves maybe slightly burnt out by the end of it.

We forget that sometimes simplicity is better than complication. Have you sat down with your family for a simple lunch meal lately? You don't have to talk, you just have to be in each other's company and enjoying the food that is being served in front of you.

I found myself appreciating these moments more than I did running around to activities thinking that I needed something big to be worth my time. I found sitting next to my family on the couch watching my own shows while they watch theirs very rewarding. I found eating alone at my favourite restaurant while watching my favourite sitcom to be equally as enjoyable as hanging out with a group of 10 friends. I also found myself richly enjoying a long warm shower every morning and evening. It is the highlights of my day.

My point is that we need to start looking at the small things we can do each day that will bring us joy. Things that are within our control. Things that we know can hardly go wrong. This will provide some stability to gain some pleasure from. The little nuggets in the day that will not be determined by external factors such as the weather, friends bailing on us, or irritating customers.

When we focus on the little things, we make life that much better to live through.

Chapter 21:

Five Steps to Clarify Your Goals

Today, we're going to talk about how and why you should start clarifying your goals.
But first, let me ask you, why do you think setting clear goals is important?

Well, imagine yourself running at a really fast speed, but you don't know where you're going. You just keep running and running towards any direction without a destination in mind. What do you think will happen next? You'll be exhausted. But will you feel fulfilled? Not really. Why? Because despite running at breakneck speed and being busy, you have failed to identify an end point. Without it, you won't know how far or near you are to where you are supposed to be. The same analogy applies to how we live our lives. No matter how productive you are or how fast your pacing is, at the end the race, if you don't have clear goals, you will simply end up wondering what the whole point of running was in the first place. You might end up in a place that you didn't intend to be. Neglecting the things that are most important on you, while focusing on all the wrong things- and that is not the best way to live your life.

So, how can we change that? How can we clarify our goals so that we are sure that we are running the race we intended to all along?

1. Imagine The Ideal Version of Yourself

Try to picture the kind of person you want to be. The things you want to have. The people you want around you. The kind of life that your ideal self is living. How does your ideal-self make small and big decisions? How does he or she perceive the world? Don't limit your imagination to what you think is pleasant and acceptable in society.

Fully integrate that ideal image of yourself into your subconscious mind and see yourself filling those shoes. That is the only way that you'll be able to see it as a real person.

Remember that the best version of yourself doesn't need to be perfect. But this is your future life so dream as big as you want, and genuinely believe that you'll be able to become that person someday in the near future.

2. Identify The Gap Between Your Ideal and Present Self

Take a hard look at your current situation now and ask yourself honesty: "How far am I away now from the person I know I need to become one day? What am I lacking at present that I am not doing or acting upon? Are there any areas that I can identify that I need to work on? Are there any new habits that I need to adopt to become that person?

Be unbiased in your self-assessment as that is the only way to give yourself a clear view of knowing exactly what you need to start working on today. Be brutally honest with your self-evaluation.

It is okay to be starting from scratch if that is where are at this point. Don't be afraid of the challenge, instead embrace and prepare yourself for the journey of a lifetime. It is way worse not knowing when and where to begin than starting from nothing at all.

3. Start Making Your Action Plan

Once you have successfully identified the gap between your present self and your ideal self, start to list down all the actions you need to take and the things that need to be done. Breakdown your action plan into milestones. Make it specific, measurable and realistic. If your action plans don't work the way you think they will, don't be afraid to make new plans. Remember that your failed plans are just part of the whole journey so enjoy every moment of it. Don't be hard on yourself while you're in the process. You're a human and not a machine. Don't forget to rest and recharge from time to time. You will be more inspired and will have more energy to go through your action plan if you are taking care of yourself at the same time.

4. Set A Timeline

Now that you have identified your overarching goal and objectives, set a period of time when you think it is reasonable for a certain milestone to be completed. You don't need to be so rigid with this timeline. Instead use it as sort of a guiding light. This guide is to serve as a reminder to provide a sense of urgency to work on your goals consistently. Don't beat yourself up unnecessarily if you do not meet your milestones as you have set up. Things change and problems do come up in our lives. As long as you keep going, you're perfectly fine. Remember that it is not about how slow or how fast you get to your destination, it is about how you persevere to continue your journey.

5. Aim For Progress, Not Perfection

You are living in an imperfect world with an imperfect system. Things will never be perfect but it doesn't mean that it will be less beautiful. While you're in the process of making new goals and working on them as you go along, always make room for mistakes and adjustments. You can plan as much as you want but life has its own way of doing things. When unforeseen events take place, don't be afraid to make changes and adjustments, or start over if you must. Even though things will not always go the way you want them to, you can still be in control of choosing how you'll move forward.

As humans, we never want to be stuck. We always want to be somewhere better. But sometimes, we get lost along the way. If we have a clear picture of where we want to be, no matter how many detours we encounter, we'll always find our way to get to our destination. And you know what, sometimes those detours are what we exactly need to keep going through our journey.

Chapter 22:
10 Signs You've Outgrown Your Life

Growth can be hard, but it is necessary sometimes you outgrow your life, and understandably it is the scar you are required to stretch yourself to something you haven't been familiar with. Growth demands you to take risks and leave your comfort behind. Another important aspect is that you should be vulnerable because whenever there is growth, failure is there. Leaving your old life behind is scary, but the alternative to that is even scarier because staying in the same position for a long time can be soul-crushing. Here are ten signs that you have outgrown your life

1. You Can No Longer Relate To The People Around You

When you realize that you are surrounded by people you have nothing to talk about, it's an obvious sign that you have outgrown them. There is also a chance that you stop enjoying the activities you previously participated in and enjoyed with them, plus communication feels like a struggle. You will receive comments from your close circle that you have changed, and you won't exactly be happy with those comments but be prepared. Others telling you that you have changed should be considered a compliment. It simply means you're growing.

2. Everyone Around You Is Changing

Another sign of you outgrowing your life is that everyone around you is changing as well. If your friends and family are making all kinds of changes in their lives and you're sitting alone on some barstool, it's time to take inventory of your life. You have outgrown your old life, so now it's time to set some new goals.

3. You Have A Constant Feeling of Discontent

Constant dissatisfaction when you were previously content with the same circumstances is a huge sign of outgrowing your life. The reason could be your current life doesn't challenge you the way it once did, and when life isn't challenging, it becomes mundane, and depression creeps in. Living in discontentment is not a way to live. You should listen to your inner voice and make some changes.

4. You're Interested In Different Things

Being interested in different activities that you previously found boring and they vastly deviate from what you found interesting that simply means you are outgrowing your current life. You should follow this inclination and engage yourself in new things. It will keep your life fresh and exciting!

5. You Fantasize About Having A Different Life

Constantly dreaming about how you wish your life was a sure sign. If you were obsessed with your life, you wouldn't be consistently envisioning a different one.

Maybe you think about living in a new city, having a new job, having different relationships, and/or new hobbies.

Recognize that you've outgrown your life and make those fantasies a reality!

6. You Have New Goals That Are Vastly Different Than Your Life

Having goals and working toward them is one of the healthiest things you can do for yourself!

BUT if your new goals would change the course of your life, you've likely outgrown your life.

7. You're Bored With Your Life

You might be bored with your job or career. Maybe you're bored with your relationships and the activities you used to love.

If your days feel dull, you're ready to shake your life up!

It's one thing to feel bored here and there but being bored EVERY DAY of your life is an awful way to live and a glaringly huge sign you've outgrown your life!

8. You Feel Like You're Going Through The Motions

This is a BIG sign you've started to outgrow your life.

If you wake up every day with zero enthusiasm and move throughout the day on autopilot, you're ready for huge life changes.

I've had points in my life where I was just getting through the day simply existing. It's a depressing way to live.

Don't accept a mundane life for yourself. Make the changes necessary to get excited about your days!

9. You Start Trying To Fill A Void

Maybe you're doing it with shopping, food, alcohol, sex, etc. This one can be hard to identify because you might just think you lack discipline or control.

Take inventory of the thoughts you have when you're tempted to engage in your addiction. Are you trying to numb feelings of dissatisfaction with your life?

10. Your Vision Board Is 100% Unrelated to Any Part of Your Current Life

This was a HUGE eye-opener for me. When I created my vision board in the New Year, it was different from my life. I have since begun to take steps to make my vision board my reality.

What does your vision board look like? Is it different than your current life? If so, you've likely outgrown your life.

What can you do to start making your vision board a reality?

Chapter 23:
5 Lessons on Being Wrong

Being wrong isn't as bad as we make it out to be. I have made many mistakes, and I have discovered five major lessons from my experiences.

1. Choices that seem poor in hindsight are an indication of growth, not self-worth or intelligence. When you look back on your choices from a year ago, you should always hope to find a few decisions that seem stupid now because that means you are growing. If you only live in the safety zone where you know you can't mess up, then you'll never unleash your true potential. If you know enough about something to make the optimal decision on the first try, then you're not challenging yourself.

2. Given that your first choice is likely to be wrong, the best thing you can do is get started. The faster you learn from being wrong, the sooner you can discover what is right. Complex situations like relationships or entrepreneurship have to start before you feel ready because no one can be truly ready. The best way to learn is to start practicing.

3. Break down topics that are too big to master into smaller tasks that can be mastered. I can't look at any business and tell you what to do. Entrepreneurship is too big of a topic. But, I can look at any website and tell you how to optimize it for building an email list because that topic is small enough for me to develop some level of expertise. If you want to get better at making accurate first choices, then play in a smaller arena. As Niels Bohr, the Nobel Prize-winning physicist, famously said, "An expert is a person who has made all the mistakes that can be made in a very narrow field."

4. The time to trust your gut is when you have the knowledge or experience to back it up. You can trust yourself to make sharp decisions in areas where you already have proven expertise. For everything else, the only way to discover what works is to adopt a philosophy of experimentation.

5. The fact that failure will happen is not an excuse for expecting to fail. There is no reason to be depressed or give up simply because you will make a few wrong choices. Even more crucial, you must try your best every time because the effort and the practice drive the learning process. They are essential, even if you fail. Realize that no single choice is destined to fail, but that occasional failure is the cost you must pay if you want to be right. Expect to win and play like it from the outset.

Your first choice is rarely the optimal choice. Make it now, stop judging yourself, and start growing.

Chapter 24:

How To Rid Yourself of Distraction

Distraction and disaster sound rather similar.
It is a worldwide disorder that you are probably suffering from.
Distraction is robbing you of precious time during the day.
Distraction is robbing you of time that you should be working on your goals.
If you don't rid yourself of distraction, you are in big trouble.

It is a phenomenon that most employees are only productive 3 out of 8 hours at the office.
If you could half your distractions, you could double your productivity.
How far are you willing to go to combat distraction?
How badly do you want to achieve proper time management?

If you know you only have an hour a day to work, would it help keep you focused?

Always focus on your initial reason for doing work in the first place.
After all that reason is still there until you reach your goal.

Create a schedule for your day to keep you from getting distracted.
Distractions are everywhere.
It pops up on your phone.

It pops up from people wanting to chat at work.
It pops up in the form of personal problems.
Whatever it may be, distractions are abound.

The only cure is clear concentration.
To have clear concentration it must be something you are excited about.
To have clear knowledge that this action will lead you to something exciting.

If you find the work boring, It will be difficult for you to concentrate too long.
Sometimes it takes reassessing your life and admitting your work is boring for you to consider a change in direction.

Your goal will have more than one path.
Some paths boring, some paths dangerous, some paths redundant, and some paths magical.
You may not know better until you try.
After all the journey is everything.

If reaching your goal takes decades of work that makes you miserable, is it really worth it?
The changes to your personality may be irreversible.

Always keep the goal in mind whilst searching for an enjoyable path to attain it.

After all if you are easily distracted from your goal, then do you really want it?

Ask yourself the hard questions.
Is this something you really want? Or is this something society wants for you?

Many people who appear successful to society are secretly miserable.
Make sure you are aware of every little detail of your life.
Sit down and really decide what will make you happy at the end of your life.

What work will you be really happy to do?
What are the causes and people you would be happy to serve?
How much money you want?
What kind of relationships you want?
If you can build a clear vision of this life for you, distractions will become irrelevant.
Irrelevant because nothing will be able to distract you from your perfect vision.

Is what you are doing right now moving you towards that life?
If not stop, and start doing the things what will.
It really is that simple.

Anyone who is distracted for too long from the task in hand has no business doing that task. They should instead be doing something that makes them happy.

We can't be happy all the time otherwise we wouldn't be able to recognize it.
But distraction is a clear indicator you may not be on the right path for you.
Clearly define your path and distraction will be powerless.

Chapter 25:

7 Habits To Do Everyday

In the words of Aristotle, *we are what we repeatedly do. Excellence then is not an act, but a habit.* An act that we repeat eventually becomes ingrained in us; it forms part of our culture and lifestyle. We speak, think and act out of the abundance of our hearts.

Here are 7 habits to do every day:

1. Praying

You have heard of the saying that an apple a day keeps the doctor away; but I dare pose to you, a prayer a day keeps the devil away. Praying is not an act for the religious or spiritual. Regardless of your faith, prayer is a pop-up notification in our lives that cannot be put off no matter how often we snooze it.

It has nothing to do with divinity but the humanity in us. Only in prayer can we be vulnerable without fear of it being used against us. We surrender our mortality to the immortal one. Prayer psyches our morale and gives us the confidence to face the uncertainty of tomorrow.

Before talking to mortals, talk to the supernatural in prayer. In solitude, you can only do so much. Prayer provides the much-needed avenue to vent to someone at the other end of the line – God.

2. Reading

Great leaders are readers (read that again). Reading widens our knowledge base and we stay up to date in current affairs. Being among the wisest of his generation, Haile Selassie says *A man who says "I have learned enough and will learn no further" should be considered as knowing nothing at all.*

Knowledge is power. Amass yourself as much of it as possible. Read newspapers and lifestyle magazines to catch up with the fast-moving world, read inspirational and motivational blogs and articles to be inspired to dream bigger, and read business magazines to be at par with innovations that will blow up your mind.

Reading gives you immeasurable exposure. Challenge yourself to read at least two books (even e-books) in one month and watch yourself grow.

3. Cleaning

Cleanliness is next to godliness. It is supposed to be a routine activity, not one to be scheduled to be done on particular days only. There is this misconception, especially in Africa, that cleaning is a gender role. No, it is not. It is everyone's responsibility to keep their immediate environment clean and not delegate it to another person, for there is only so much that they can do.

Most people fail at this because they keep postponing cleaning duties. Why do it later when you can do it now? Do your laundry, wash your utensils, clean your kitchen, take shower, dust off your working space at the office, routinely dust off your laptop or desktop, get a clean shave (for the gents) every so often to maintain your facial hair too, and even dust off seats before you sit down. Do not wait for someone else to take responsibility for your cleanliness. It is a sign of irresponsibility on your part.

Cleanliness has immense benefits. Do you remember how you felt after taking that warm bath at the end of your busy day? How well were you received at your workstation when you showed up clean-shaven and well-groomed? Embracing cleanliness will open doors that character alone cannot.

4. Being Kind

A person's character is known from how they treat strangers, hotel attendants, public service vehicle operators, the needy in the streets, and those who have no means to repay them. Kindness is a habit, not an occasional act.

Make a point of being kind to those you meet every day. Do to others what you would like to be done to you. Karma is there to equalize the math. Kindness has no affiliation with being religious (although it is a doctrine in religion), but it is about being a better person. If you can donate to that charity event, do it generously. If you can clear the hospital bill of the sick, do it willingly. If you can pay fees for the needy students, kindly step in.

Make kindness your habit and generosity a part of you. It is not to mean that you become irrationally kind. Use rational judgment to distinguish between genuine and fake needy people. A simple act of kindness will change someone's life.

5. Planning

If you fail to plan, you are planning to fail. Planning arises from simple ignorable things. The not-so-petty matters that we overlook and comfort ourselves by saying it will not happen again. How often have we done impulse buying when shopping? It may look trivial but its impact on our finances cannot be overlooked.

Get your acts together and prioritize planning. Earn before you spend and save after you earn. Failure to plan will drive you to bankruptcy and depression. A good plan is a job half done. When you anticipate what will come next, you will be prepared to handle it effectively. That is what planning does to a man. It makes you a semi-god with the ability to come up with solutions to problems that are yet to come but are around the corner.

Isn't it adorable how powerful planning is? It is neither tedious as many see it nor reserved for the elite. A plan is essential for personal success.

6. Learn Something New

Knowledge is power. The best gift you can give yourself is to widen your knowledge base. Learn life hacks, human psychology and socializing. There are those lessons which cannot be taken in a classroom but out there in the real world. Take it upon yourself to learn something new daily.

Nothing is stagnant in the current world. Walk with the changes lest you be left behind. Adapt to new practices in your industry fast enough before most people do. Your flexibility will bring something to the table and you will attract greatness.

Learning something new daily is not solely academic. Regardless of your level of education, there is always something to learn. Do not despise those below you in the social ladder, you can always learn a thing or two.

7. Talk To At Least One Stranger

We all are reluctant to talk to strangers for one reason or another. We are worried about how they will respond to our greetings or maybe our proposals. One thing however is clear – strangers could be the potential turning point of our businesses and jobs. They could be the breakthrough we have been waiting for.

Pick up the courage to greet a stranger today and further a conversation. Be warned that some could be opportunists and exploit your goodwill. Nevertheless, talk to a stranger. Greet the people you find at the bus stage and the security guard at your place.

These 7 habits to do everyday are essential for personal growth.

Chapter 26: Enjoying The Journey

Today I want to talk about why enjoying the journey of life is important. And why hurrying to get to the destination might not be all that enjoyable as we think it is.

A lot of us plan our lives around an end goal, whether it be getting to a particular position in our company's ladder, or becoming the best player in a sport, or having the most followers on Instagram or whatever the goal may be... Many of us just can't wait to get there. However, many a times, once we reach our goal, whilst we may feel a sense of satisfaction and accomplishment for a brief moment, we inevitably feel like something is missing again and we search for our next objective and target to hit.

I have come to realise that in life, it is not always so much the end goal, but the journey, trials, struggles, and tribulations that make the journey there worth it. If we only focus on the end goal, we may miss out the amazing sights along the way. We will ultimately miss the point of the journey and why we embarked on it in the first place.

Athletes who achieve one major title never stop at just that one, they look for the next milestone they can achieve, but they enjoy the process, they take it one step at a time and at the end of their careers they can look back with joy that they had left no stone unturned. And that they can live their life without regret.

How many times have you seen celebrities winning the biggest prize in their careers, whether it may be the Grammy's Album of the Year if you are a musician, or the Oscars Best Actor or Best Actress Award. How many of them actually feel like that is the end of the journey? They keep creating and keep making movies and film not because they want that award, even though it is certainly a nice distinction to have, but more so because they enjoy their craft and they enjoy the art of producing.

If winning that trophy was the end goal, we would see many artists just end their careers there and then after reaching the summit. However that is not the case. They will try to create something new for as long as people are engaged with their craft, as with the case of Meryl Streep, even at 70+ she is still working her butt off even after she has achieve all the fame and money in the world.

Even for myself, at times i just want to reach the end as quickly as possible. But many times when i get there, i am never satisfied. I feel empty inside and i feel that I should be doing more. And when i rush to the end, i do feel like I missed many important sights along the way that would have made the journey much more rewarding and enjoyable had I told myself to slow it down just a little.

I believe that for all of us, the journey is much more important than the destination. It is through the journey that we grow as a person, it is through the journey that we evolve and take on new ideas, work ethics, knowledge, and many little nuggets that make the trip worth it at the end. If someone were to hand you a grand slam title without having you earned it, it would be an empty trophy with no meaning and emotions behind it. The trophy would not represent the hours of hard work that you have put in to be deserving of that title.

So I challenge each and everyone of you today to take a step back in whatever journey you may be on. To analyse in what aspects can you enjoy the moment and to not place so much pressure into getting to the destination asap. Take it one day at a time and see how the journey you are on is actually a meaningful one that you should treasure each day and not let up.

Chapter 27:

Do You Know What You Want?

Do you know who you are? Do you know what you are? Do you know what you want to become? Do you have any idea what you might become?

Every sane human has asked these questions to themselves multiple times in their lives. We have a specific trait of always finding the right answers to everything. We humans always try to find the meaning behind everything.

It's in our built-in nature to question everything around us. Yet we are here in this modern era of technology and resources and we don't have a sense of purpose. We don't have a true set of goals. We don't give enough importance to our future to take a second and make a long-term plan for longer gains.

The fault in our thinking is that we don't have a strict model of attention. We have too many distractions in our lives to spare a moment to clear our minds.

The other thing that makes us confused or ignorant is the fact that people have a way of leading us into thinking things that are not ours to start with.

Society has made these norms that have absolutely nothing to do with anyone except that these were someone's experience when they were once at our stage. We are dictated on things that are not ours to achieve but only a mere image of what others want us to achieve or don't.

No one has the right to tell you anything. No one has a right to say anything to you except if they are advising or reminding you of the worst. But to inflict a scenario with such surety that it will eventually happen to you because you have a fault that many others had before you is the most superstitious and illogical thing to do on any planet let alone Earth.
No one knows what the future holds for anyone. No one can guarantee even the next breath that they take. So why put yourself under someone else's spell of disappointment? Why do you feel the need to satisfy every person's whim? Why do you feel content with everyone around you getting their ways?

You always know in your heart, deep down in some corner what you want. You will always know what you need to be fulfilled. You will always find an inspiration within yourself to go and pursue that thing. What you need are some self-confidence and some self-motivation. You need to give yourself some time to straighten up your thoughts and you will eventually get the BOLD statement stating 'This is what I want'.

You don't need to shut everyone around you. You just need to fix your priorities and you will get a vivid image of what things are and what they can become.

There is no constraint of age or gender to achieving anything. These are just mental and emotional hurdles that we have imposed on our whole race throughout our history.

Just remember. When you know what you want, and you want it bad enough to give away everything for that, you will someday find a way to finally get it.

Chapter 28:
6 Ways To Adopt A Better Lifestyle For Long-Term Success

A good lifestyle leads to a good life. The important choices we make throughout our lives impact our future in numerous ways. The need to make ourselves better in every aspect of life and the primary ability to perform such a routine can be a lifestyle. There is no proper way to live written in a book; however, through our shared knowledge and our comprehension, we can shape a lifestyle that can be beneficial and exciting at the same time. Though there is no doubt that falling into a specific routine can be difficult but, maintaining a proper state is more critical for a successful life.

For long-term success, a good lifestyle is a priority. Almost everything we do in our lives directly or indirectly involves our future self. So, a man needs to become habitual of such things that can profit him in every way possible. To visualize a better you, You need to configure just about everything around you. And to change all the habits that may make you feel lagging. The most common feature of a better lifestyle for long-term success is determination.

1. Change In Pattern Of Your Life

It is good to shape a pattern of living from the start and forming good habits, engaging yourself in profitable practice, and choosing a healthier custom. It feels impossible to change something you have already been habitual of, but willpower is the key. With some motivation and dedication, you can change yourself into a better version of yourself. You are choosing what might be suitable for you and staying determined on that thought. The first step is to let go of harmful things slowly because letting go of habits and patterns that you are used to can be challenging. After some, sometime you will notice yourself letting go of things more easily.

2. Take Your Time

Time is an essential factor when it comes to forming a lifestyle for a successful life. Time can seem to slow through the process, making us think that it may have been stopped in our most difficult moments. Similarly, making us feel it goes flying by when our life is relaxed and at ease. Time never stops for anyone. It is crucial to make sure we make most of our time and consume it in gaining more knowledge and power. Take time to inform your lifestyle, but not more than required. We are taking things at a moderate pace so you can both enjoy life and do work.

3. Don't Always Expect Things To Go Your Way

As much as we humans like to get our hopes high, we can't always expect things to go our way. Even things we have worked hard for can sometimes go downhill. It is at times overconfidence, but sometimes it can be pure bad luck. We can't get disheartened by something that was not meant to go a specific way. Don't expect perfection in all the work you do. Staying patient is the walk towards the reward. And making the best out of the worst can be the only way to get yourself going.

4. Don't Be Afraid To Ask For Help

It is human nature to ask each other for help now and then. If it comes to this point, don't be afraid to ask for help yourself. Ask someone superior to aid you on matters you find difficult. Don't hesitate to ask your inferiors who might have more knowledge than you in some certain customs. Help them, too, if needed. Ask them to assist you out on points, but never make them do the whole project. Don't make someone do something you wouldn't do yourself.

5. Be Prompt In Everything

Lagging behind your work can be the worst possible habit you could raise. Make yourself punctual in every aspect. Make sure you are on time everywhere. Either it's to wake up in the morning or to go to a meeting. Laziness can never be proven good for you or your dream towards a prosperous lifestyle. Respect time, and it shall respect you. Show your colleges that they can depend on you to show up on time and take responsibility for work. You would rather wait than making others wait for you. That will show you seriousness toward your business.

6. Keep A Positive Attitude

Keeping a positive attitude can lead to a positive lifestyle. Be happy with yourself in every context, and make sure that everything you do has your complete confidence. Be thankful to all who surround you. Keep a positive attitude, whether it be a home or office. Speak with your superiors with respect and make yourself approachable around inferiors. Your positive mindset can affect others in a way too. They will become more inclined towards you, and they can easily suggest you help someone.

Conclusion

Just about everything in your life affects your future in a way or other, so make sure that you do all you can to make yourself worth the praise. Keep your lifestyle simple but effective. Try to do as much as possible for yourself and make time to relax as well. For long-term success, willpower is the most important; make sure you have it. Keep your headlight and calm for the upcoming difficulties and prepare yourself to face almost everything life throws at you.

Chapter 29:
Being 100% Happy Is Overrated

Lately I've been feeling as though happiness isn't something that truly lasts. Happiness isn't something that will stay with us very long. We may feel happy when we are hanging out with friends, but that feeling will eventually end once we part for the day. I've been feeling as though expecting to be constantly happy is very overrated. We try to chase this idea of being happy. We chase the material possessions, we chase the fancy cars, house, and whatever other stuff that we think will make us happy. But more often than not the desire is never really fulfilled. Instead, i believe that the feeling accomplishment is a much better state of mind to work towards. Things will never make us happy. We may enjoy the product we have worked so hard for temporarily. But that feeling soon goes away. And we are left wondering what is the next best thing we can aim our sights on. This never-ending chase becomes a repetitive cycle, one that we never truly are aware of but constantly desire. We fall into the trap that finding happiness is the end all-be-all.

What i've come to realise is that most of the time, we are actually operating on a more baseline level. A state that is skewed more towards the neutral end. Neither truly happy, or neither truly sad. And I believe that is perfectly okay. We should allow ourselves to embrace and accept the fact that it is okay to be just fine. Just neutral. Sure it isn't something very exciting, but we shouldn't put ourselves in a place where we expect to be constantly happy in order to lead a successful life. This revelation came when I realised that every time I felt happy, I would experience a crash in mood the next day. I would start looking at instagram, checking up on my friends, comparing their days, and thinking that they are leading a happier life than I was. I would then start berating myself and find ways to re-create those happy moments just for the sake of it. Just because I thought i needed to feel happy all the time. It was only when I actually sat down and started looking inwards did I realise that maybe I can never truly find happiness from external sources.

Instead of trying to find happiness in things and external factors that are beyond my control, I started looking for happiness from within myself. I began to appreciate how happy I was simply being alone. Being by myself. Not letting other factors pull me down. I found that I was actually happiest when I was taking a long shower, listening to my own thoughts. No music playing, no talking to people, just me typing away on my computer, writing down all the feelings I am feeling, all the thoughts that I am thinking, letting every emotion I was feeling out of my system. I started to realise that the lack of distractions, noise, comparisons with others, free from social media, actually provided me with a clearer mind. It was in those brief moments where I found myself to be my most productive, with ideas streaming all over the place. It was in that state of mind that I did feel somewhat happy. That I could create that state of mind without depending on other people to fulfil it for me.

If any of you out there feel that your emotions are all over the place, maybe it is time for you to sit down by yourself for a little while. Stop searching for happiness in things and stuff, and sometimes even people. We think it is another person's job to make us happy. We expect to receive compliments, flowers, a kiss, in order to feel happy. While those things are certainly nice to have, being able to find happiness from within is much better. By sitting and reflecting in a quiet space, free from any noise and distractions, we may soon realise that maybe we are okay being just okay. Maybe we don't need expensive jewellery or handbags or fancy houses to make us happy. Maybe we just need a quiet mind and a grateful spirit.

The goal is to find inner peace. To accept life for the way it is. To accept things as the way they are. To be grateful for the things we have. That is what it means to be happy.

Chapter 30:

Five Habits of A Joy-Filled Marriage

The institution of marriage is one shrouded in mystery. One that is so deep that even married couples have a hard time adjusting to it. Numerous divorces are filled at courts of law albeit the fact that these weddings were full of pomp and color. Nevertheless, some marriages have withstood the test of time despite facing several challenges.

Here are five habits of a joy-filled marriage:

1. **Open Communication**

Communication is the master key to unlocking joy in marriage. A majority of unions that have been annulled were caused by a communication breakdown. What holds you from communicating with your marriage partner?

There is the fear of your better half being judgmental when you express your concerns. It ought not to be the case. You should be able to speak freely with your partner. The purpose of communication is to understand his/her expectations and let them know yours too. When this fails, conflicts are bound to arise.

Prevention is better than cure. It is wise to iron out any potential areas of conflict before they arise. Open communication is fearlessly talking to your partner about issues the moment they surface in your marriage. It is unhealthy to suppress any discontentment you may have. Use diplomacy - founded in communication - to unlock joy. A couple can talk to each other about their deepest desires and worst fears if there is healthy communication between them. One is capable of fulfilling his/her partner's wishes because they know them well.

2. Selflessness

Marriage is a union where two adults become one. The two are supposed to take care of each other and see themselves through thick and thin. This is impossible if either the husband or wife is selfish.

Selflessness is putting the needs of your partner ahead of your own. Who does not love to be well-taken care of? Your partner too does. In showing love to him/her, joy blossoms. Joy is found when the couple is happy with each other. The essence of marriage is to have a partner with whom you will share your life selflessly.

Tranquility prevails in marriage when both parties see the effort that the other is investing in. It is a show of commitment towards the success of the marriage. Invite joy in your marriage by being selflessly committed to it. It sets a good example for your family. Your children will grow up into responsible adults with the right values from a young age. That is the beauty of marriage.

3. Pursue Common Goals

Two cannot walk together unless they agree. A married couple should share a common vision for them to read from the same page as they build their home together. When a couple is divided, the marriage will collapse. Joy in marriage is attained when a couple pursues common goals. They become each other's best friend and confidant. Conflict arises when the couple cannot agree on what to do jointly and subsequently, joy becomes a mirage if they cannot work towards a common purpose. In place of joy, grief reigns.

The dream of every couple is to have a joy-filled marriage. This will remain an illusion if the couple does not commit to a common goal. Marriage is a work in progress; there is room to develop common goals to pursue as a couple. It is never late.

4. Have Mutual Respect

Love forms a marriage but mutual respect holds it together. It is the glue that keeps a couple together in the eternal union. Joy is not guaranteed in marriage but is cultivated by the couple having mutual respect.

They will never insult each other in public or private. There is a golden rule in marriage - defend your partner in public but correct them in private. You should ensure that the public image of your partner is as clean as possible and always step up in areas of their deficiency. Anything that affects them directly touches you.

When your partner sees the concern you have for their image, they will return the respect which you have rightfully earned. This kind of relationship in marriage nurtures love and joy. Mutual respect will restrict you from making fun of or interfering with your partner's beliefs. These boundaries will be available when your relationship with your partner is healthy.

5. Do Things Together

You must develop the habit of doing things together as a couple. This simple routine will make you bond more and get to understand your partner better. The blessings of an overflow of joy will be your portion in marriage.

When you do things together with your partner, it signifies your concern and love for each other because you do not want them to be overwhelmed. Moreover, you save time when you combine efforts.

These are the five habits of a joy-filled marriage. Incorporate them into your marriage and enjoy joy at its peak.

Chapter 31:
How To Succeed In Life

"You can't climb the ladder of success with your hands in your pocket."

Every day that you're living, make a habit of making the most out of it. Make a habit of winning today. Don't dwell on the past, don't worry about the future. You just have to make sure that you're winning today. Move a little forward every day; take a little step every day. And when you're giving your fruitful efforts, you're making sure you're achieving your day, then you start to built confidence within yourselves. Confidence is when you close your eyes at night and see a vision, a dream, a goal, and you believe that you're going to achieve it. When you're doing things, when you're productive the whole day, then that long journey will become short in a matter of time.

Make yourself a power list for each day. Take a sheet of paper, write Monday on top of it and then write five critical, productive, actionable tasks that you're going to do that day. After doing the task, cross it off. Repeat the process every day of every week of every month till you get closer to achieving your goals, your dreams. It doesn't matter if you're doing the same tasks every day or how minor or major they are; what matters is that it's creating momentum in things that you've believed you couldn't do. And as soon as the momentum gets completed, you start to believe that you can do something. You eventually stop writing your tasks down because now they've become your new habits. You need a reminder for them. You don't need to cross them off because you're going to do them. The power list helps you win the day. You're stepping out of your comfort zone, doing something that looks uncomfortable for starters, but while doing this, even for a year, you will see yourself standing five years from where you're standing today.

Decide, commit, act, succeed, repeat. If you want to be an inspiration to others, a motivator to others, impact others somehow, you have to self-evaluate certain perceptions and think that'll help you change the way you see yourself and the world. Perseverance, hard-working, and consistency would be the keywords if one were to achieve success in life. You just have to keep yourself focused on your ultimate goal. You will fall a hundred times. There's always stumbling on the way. But if you have the skill, the power, the instinct to get yourself back up every time you fall, and to dig yourself out of the whole, then no one can stop you. You have to control the situation, Don't ever let the situation control you. You're living life exactly as it should be. If you don't like what you're living in, then consider changing the aspects. The person you are right now versus the person you want to be in the future, there's only a fine line between the two that you have to come face-to-face with.

Your creativity is at most powerful the moment you open your eyes and start your day. That's when you get the opportunity to steer your emotions and thoughts in the direction that you want them to go, not the other way around. Every failure is a step closer to success. We won't succeed on the first try, and we will never have it perfect by trying it only once. But we can master the art of not giving up. We dare to take risks. If we never fail, we never get the chance of getting something we never had. We can never taste the fruits of success without falling. The difference between successful people and those who aren't successful is the point of giving up.

Success isn't about perfection. Instead, it's about getting out of bed each day, clearing the dust off you, and thinking like a champion, a winner, going on about your day, being productive, and making the most out of it. Remember that the mind controls your body; your body doesn't hold your mind. You have to make yourself mentally tough to overcome the fears and challenges that come in the way of your goals. As soon as you get up in the morning, start thinking about anything or anyone that you're grateful for. Your focus should be on making yourself feel good and confident enough to get yourself through the day.

The negative emotions that we experience, like pain or rejection, or frustration, cannot always make our lives miserable. Instead, we can consider them as our most incredible friends that'll drive us to success. When people succeed, they tend to party. When they fail, they tend to ponder. And the pondering helps us get the most victories in our lives. You're here, into another day, still breathing fine, that means you got another chance, to better yourself, to be able to right your wrongs. Everyone has a more significant potential than the roles they put themselves in.

Trust yourself always. Trust your instinct—no matter what or how anyone thinks. You're perfectly capable of doing things your way. Even if they go wrong, you always learn something from them. Don't ever listen to the naysayers. You've probably heard a million times that you can't do this and you can't do that, or it's never even been done before. So what? So what if no one has ever done it before. That's more of the reason for you to do it since you'll become the first person to do it. Change that 'You can't' into 'Yes, I definitely can.' Muhammad Ali, one of the greatest boxers to walk on the face of this planet, was once asked, 'how many sit-ups do you do?' to which he replied, 'I don't count my sit-ups. I only start counting when it starts hurting. When I feel pain, that's when I start counting because that's when it really counts.' So we get a wonderful lesson to work tirelessly and shamelessly if we were to achieve our dreams. Dr. Arnold Schwarzenegger beautifully summed up life's successes in 6 simple rules; Trust yourself, Break some rules, Don't be afraid to fail, Ignore the naysayers, Work like hell, And give something back.

Chapter 32: Learning To Trust Others

Today we're going to talk about a topic that has the potential to make or break your working relationships or personal relationships with others.

Trust is something that consistently ranks on the top of relationship goals and it has very good reasons for that. Without trust there is basically no foundation. When you can't trust someone, it basically means that you don't believe they can be left alone without your supervision. If you don't trust someone to do the work you have passed along to them, basically it means you are either micro-managing them all day long or that you might just end up doing the work entirely yourself because you don't believe that they can do a job up to your expectations. How many of you have experienced bosses who are micro-managers like that? Basically it either means that they think they can do a better job or that they don't trust you to do the work at all. And we all hate bosses who are like that. Look into mirror like that now, are you doing that to someone at your workplace now?

If you don't trust someone in a relationship, basically you don't believe that they can't be left to their own devices either if they are out of your sight. You start to worry about what they might do when you're gone. If a partner has cheated on you before, I bet that trust has probably gone out the window and it might take a lot of time and energy to actually start trusting that person again. If you don't trust a friend, you might not want to tell them secrets for fear that they may go round sharing it with others without your consent. That plays into the concept of trustworthiness as well. It all comes in a package.

To build trust, we have to earn it. With our actions we can show others that we can be trusted with information, secrets, work, to be faithful, and to do right thing at all times. But trust works both ways as well. If we want people to trust us, we must be willing to extend the trust to others as well. If others have displayed level of competency, we need to start learning to trust that they can get the work done without breathing down their necks all times of the day. If however they come back with shoddy work, maybe you might want to keep a closer eye on them before you feel that their work is up to your standards.

Let others prove to you otherwise by giving them the benefit of the doubt first and then assessing their abilities after.

When you show others that you trust them to do a task, more often than not they will feel a sense of urgency and responsibility to get the work done properly and promptly so that they can show you that they are capable. To show you that they are competent and worthy of the trust that you have placed in them. When you can learn to trust can you truly let go and live life freely. Always having to micro-manage others can not only hurt your reputation as "that guy" but also allow you to have more time do focus on areas where your attention is really required. When you can learn to trust can you truly expand and grow a team, business, company, friendships, and relationships.

I challenge each and everyone of you to learn to trust others and not feel like you have to manage everyone around you to the granular level. If you feel that you have trust issues, for whatever reason, consider working on it or maybe even seeking help. Trust issues usually stems from a past traumatic event or experience that may have impacted your ability to trust again. If so you may one to dig deeper to discover the root of the problem and work through it till the feeling goes away.

CPSIA information can be obtained
at www.ICGtesting.com
Printed in the USA
LVHW052148120422
716027LV00016B/615